AF432661

Date:

Created especially for you

Date:

Created especially for you

Date:

Created especially for you

Date: _______________________

Created especially for you

Date:

Created especially for you

Date:

Created especially for you

Date:

Created especially for you

Date:

Created especially for you

Date: ______________________

Created especially for you

Date:

Created especially for you

Date:

Created especially for you

Date:

Created especially for you

Date:

Created especially for you

Date:

Created especially for you

Date:

Date:

Created especially for you

Created especially for you

Date:

Date: ________________________

Created especially for you

Date:

Created especially for you

Date: ____________________

Created especially for you

Date:

Created especially for you

Date: ______________________________

Created especially for you

Date:

Created especially for you

Date: _______________________

Created especially for you

Date:

Created especially for you

Date:

Created especially for you

Date:

Created especially for you

Date:

Created especially for you

Date: ____________________

Created especially for you

Date:

Created especially for you

Date:

Created especially for you

Date:

Date: _______________________

Created especially for you

Date: _______________

Created especially for you

Date: ___________________________

Created especially for you

Date:

Created especially for you

Date: _______________________

Created especially for you

Date:

Created especially for you

Date:

Created especially for you

Date:

Created especially for you

Date: _______________________

Created especially for you

Date:

Created especially for you

Date:

Created especially for you

Date:

Created especially for you

Date: ______________________________

Created especially for you

Date:

Created especially for you

Date:

Created especially for you

Date:

Created especially for you

Date:

Date: ___________________________

Created especially for you

Date:

Created especially for you

Date: ______________________________

Created especially for you

Date:

Created especially for you

Date: _______________________

Created especially for you

Date:

Created especially for you

Date:

Created especially for you

Date:

Created especially for you

Date: _______________________________

Created especially for you

Date:

Created especially for you

Date:

Created especially for you

Date:

Created especially for you

Date:

Created especially for you

Date:

Created especially for you

Date:

Created especially for you

Date:

Created especially for you

Date: _______________________________

Created especially for you

Date:

Created especially for you

Date:

Created especially for you

Date:

Created especially for you

Date: _______________

Created especially for you

Date:

Date:

Date:

Created especially for you

Date: _______________________________

Created especially for you

Date:

Created especially for you

Date:

Created especially for you

Date:

Created especially for you

Date:

Date:

Date: _______________________________

Created especially for you

Date:

Created especially for you

Date:

Created especially for you

Date:

Date:

Date:

Created especially for you

Date: _______________________

Date: _______________________

Created especially for you

Date:

Created especially for you

Date:

Created especially for you

Date:

Date:

Created especially for you

Date:

Date:

Date:

Created especially for you

Date:

Created especially for you

Date:

Created especially for you

Date:

Created especially for you

Date: ___________________________

Created especially for you

Date: ______________________________

Created especially for you

Date:

Created especially for you

Date:

Created especially for you

Date: _______________________

Created especially for you

Date:

Date:

Created especially for you

Date:

Created especially for you

Date:

Created especially for you

Date:

Created especially for you

Date:

Created especially for you

Date:

Date: _______________________________

Created especially for you

Date:

Created especially for you

Date: _______________________________

Date:

Created especially for you

Date: _______________________

Created especially for you

Date: ___________________________

Created especially for you

Date:

Created especially for you

Date:

Created especially for you

Date:

Date:

Created especially for you

Date:

Date:

Created especially for you

Date:

Created especially for you

Date:

Created especially for you

Date: _______________________

Created especially for you

Date:

Created especially for you

Date:

Created especially for you

Date: _______________________________

Created especially for you

Date:

Created especially for you

Date: _______________________

Created especially for you

Date:

Date: _______________________________

Created especially for you

Date:

Created especially for you

Date:

Created especially for you

Date:

Date: ______________________________

Date:

Created especially for you

Date:

Created especially for you

Date:

Created especially for you

Date: _______________________________

Created especially for you

Date:

Date: _______________

Created especially for you

Date:

Created especially for you

Date: _______________________________

Created especially for you

Date:

Created especially for you

Date:

Created especially for you

Date:

Created especially for you

Date:

Created especially for you

Date:

Created especially for you

Date: _______________________

Created especially for you

Date:

Created especially for you

Date:

Date:

Date:

Created especially for you

Date:

Created especially for you

Date: _______________________________

Created especially for you

Date:

Created especially for you

Date: _______________________

Created especially for you

Date:

Created especially for you

Date:

Created especially for you

Date:

Created especially for you

Date:

Date:

Created especially for you

Date: _______________________

Date:

Created especially for you

Date: _______________________

Created especially for you

Date:

Created especially for you

Date:

Created especially for you

Date:

Created especially for you

Date:

Created especially for you

Date:

Created especially for you

Date: _______________________________

Created especially for you

Date:

Created especially for you

Date: _______________________

Created especially for you

Date:

Created especially for you

Date: _______________________________

Created especially for you

Date:

Created especially for you

Date: _______________________

Created especially for you

Date:

Created especially for you

Date: _______________________

Created especially for you

Date:

Date:

Created especially for you

Date:

Created especially for you

Date: ___________________________

Created especially for you

Date:

Created especially for you

Date: ____________________

Created especially for you

Date:

Created especially for you

Date: ____________________

Created especially for you

Date:

Created especially for you

Date: ___________________________________

Created especially for you

Date: _______________________

Created especially for you

Date: _______________________________

Created especially for you

Date:

Created especially for you

Date:

www.ingramcontent.com/pod-product-compliance
Lightning Source LLC
Chambersburg PA
CBHW071511140726
47997CB00005B/1936